To: Aditi

From: Momy

**Also by Ashley Rice**

*girls rule*
*Love Is Me and You*
*You Are an Amazing Girl*
*You Go, Girl... Keep Dreaming*

Library of Congress Control Number: 2005905355
ISBN: 1-59842-065-8

Certain trademarks are used under license.
BLUE MOUNTAIN PRESS is registered in U.S. Patent and Trademark Office.

Printed in the United States of America.
First Printing: 2006

 This book is printed on recycled paper.

This book is printed on fine quality, laid embossed, 80 lb. paper. This paper has been specially produced to be acid free (neutral pH) and contains no groundwood or unbleached pulp. It conforms with the requirements of the American National Standards Institute, Inc., so as to ensure that this book will last and be enjoyed by future generations.

# Blue Mountain Arts, Inc.

P.O. Box 4549, Boulder, Colorado 80306

# Thanks for Being My Friend

a special book
to celebrate friendship
with someone very important... you

Ashley Rice

**Blue Mountain Press**™

Boulder, Colorado

Friends are angels sent
down to earth to make
good days and to help
us find our way.

Thanks for being my friend.

Friends like you
are hard to find.
In a lifetime you get
only a few.
And when you find them,
you always know
them by sight and
by heart alone.
And when you find them,
you always grow
a little bit taller
in your soul.

And when you find
them, you also know
that as the years
come and as the years
go by... you have
been blessed just
to know them;
thus blessed am I,
thus lucky have
I been...
to know a friend
like you.

# You Are My Anchor

You are my anchor
  in this world
and in these rough
    and crazy seas.
When hearts and hopes
go down like ships,
you help me hold on
  to my dreams.

When other parts
   of me have gone,
you keep me going.
You keep me sane.
You are the treasure
   I love most, like an
umbrella in the rain.
You are my anchor in
   this world, from here to as
far as I can see...

   You are my anchor
      in this world, and that
      means everything
         to me.

You Have a Friend in Me Forever

You'll have a friend in me
if there's a time when you're
feeling down.
You'll have a friend in me —
I'll stand beside you —
I'll come around.

And you'll have a friend
in me when you're shining
and at your best,
or when things are moving
way too slow...
or maybe just too fast.

You'll **have** a friend in me
from the start...
and **until** the end...
you'll have a place
in my **heart** —
because I'm proud to
call you my friend.

You believed in me when
I wasn't that strong.
You held my hand.
You let me be wrong.
You laughed with me
when my jokes weren't
that funny, stood by me when
I had no money.

You lent me your heart...
You lent me your hand...
from the start, you were
my friend...
funny how life brings
us rainbows and very
special people when
we need them the most.

# ...And I Believe in You, Too

I **believe** in the way that you are
and the way you will **be**.
I believe in the things that you say.
You mean the world to me.
And if you should go,
if you should **turn around** one day,
if you should ever doubt your dreams
in any way,
don't think twice about it.
Don't **worry** too long
about whether you'll find a **place**
for yourself in the world —
**you belong.**

I know that you'll get where
you're going someday.
For no matter what happens,
you will find a way.
I believe in the way that you
are and the way you will be.
You are a shining star
in this world...

and you mean the world
to me.

Sometimes I wonder if you know how wonderful you are, or if being wonderful is one of those things that somebody has to tell you about, like when everyone is talking about how beautiful this one person is and that one person is the only one who doesn't know.

Maybe you already know how wonderful you are on the inside, but as your friend, I just wanted to tell you that this wonderfulness of yours...

it shows.

amazing  unique

wise  funny

true  excellent  kind

understanding  talented

strong  brave

brilliant  super

...Just a few
words about
you.

Looking back over the years,
I cannot believe how many
times you stuck up for me,
stood by my side, or
helped me ride through all the
changes that life brings.

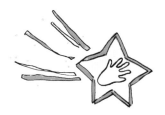

You are so dear to me... You stand by me and understand. You are like a star that guides my hand... when I need it most. And when I look back on all these years of us being friends... I wonder...

How would I ever have gotten this far without you beside me?

You are the best.

# Definition of
# a Good Friend:

A good friend is: someone who makes you smile. A good friend is: someone you're always happy to see. A good friend is: someone who is fun to hang around with, who listens, laughs, cares, shines, understands.

I think there should be an entry in the dictionary for the word(s) "good friend" (and then next to it, as the major example, could be your picture).

Some people walk into our lives with open hearts and open minds and make us see things differently. They make us learn new things and help us to live our lives more fully. Some people walk into our lives with open hearts and open minds and become our friends...

...Thank you for doing
all of these things.

There's nothing like a little help from my friends.

Thanks for being there for me...
for standing by my side... and
holding my hand. Thanks for
laughing with me... and for making
me laugh. Thanks for being there
through the good times and bad.
Thanks for staying when the sun
would not shine... and when
there were rainbows
everywhere we
chanced to
look.

There are few friends quite like you...

You say things
that I care about...

you do things
that matter...

you make a
difference
to me...

you make a difference to
other people, too...

and I know for a fact that if you were not here...

I wouldn't like the world quite as much as I do now.

# What I Learned from You

What I **learned** from you is that a **different way** of looking at things can bring hope, like rain, in times of stress.

What I learned
from you
is that getting through
situations is mostly
a matter of
perspective,
strength,
and courage.
What I learned from you
is that we often find
our best friends
in the strangest
ways and places.
What I learned from you
is friendship.

Friendship is a gift that cannot be replaced. We make friends and they change us. They enter our lives and push us to try harder. They make us be our best.

Some friendships help us to rise above our problems and those of society. Other friends seem to always be able to make us laugh...

...but either way — no matter what friendship does exactly, in a greater sense — somehow we are made kinder, better, and greater for it.
...Always.

# Without You...
# Where Would I Be?

Maybe I would
be stuck
in a tree.

Maybe I would
lose my heart
in sadness...

or maybe there
would just be
a lot less
gladness
in my life...

...from
your smile.

I don't know...
I'm just glad that
you're a part of
my days.

# Thanks for Being There

I go to you because you make me laugh and because you listen to me even if I'm tired and it takes me a while to make any sense (coherent sentences, I mean).

I go to you because you remind me of only good things; you keep a smile in your back pocket for the times that I'm upset and almost never say lame lines like "I told you so..."

I go to you because you've got a heart that matches mine, and if there were ever a time when I couldn't call on you I would be sad. You could call on me, though.

When you're standing by me I can see for miles. And having you to go to if I shine or fall makes me glad.

# 10 Things I Will Never Do:

1. I will never be too **old** to **laugh** at stupid jokes.
2. I will never be too **busy** to find time for special things that I think are important.
3. I will never **wait** in line for three hours in the **rain**.
4. I will never **break** a single person's heart, if I can help it.
5. I will never be too **sophisticated** to look for cloud shapes in the sky.

6.  I will never be too skeptical to believe in dreams, or too jaded even to try.

7.  I will never eat a vegetable dish I can't pronounce, unless there's a really good reason.

8.  I will never be so preoccupied that I forget the day or season.

9.  I will never forget all the times we got through.

10. I will never stop being friends with you.

The **shirt**
off my **back**...

the **shoes**
off my **feet**...

I'd **give**
them to you...

without missing
a **beat**.

Whenever you
**need** them...

whenever you
**call**...

my
## heart

and my
## hand

and my
## love:

take them
all.

The shirt
off my back...

my friendship
to keep...

I'd give them to you,
without missing a beat.

# I Want You to Know
# I'll Be There for You

If you've got secrets you want to tell, we can talk all day long. If your dreams get broken somehow, I'll remind you that you belong. If you need someplace to hide, you can hold my hand for a while. If your sky begins to fall, I'll stay with you 'til you smile.

Whenever you need some space, there's my room — you can take it. If someone breaks your heart, together we'll unbreak it. When you feel sad or empty inside, I'll show you you're not alone. If you get lost out there, I'll come and take you home. I'll go with you somewhere else, when you need to get away. And when nothing seems to be going right and you need a friend...

I'll stay.

You are one of the most
amazing people I know.

You do things other people
can't do.

You live your life to
the fullest.

To your own heart you
are true.

...There's no one else quite like you. And I admire you for that.

## On What They Will Say About You "Tomorrow":

There is this game people play sometimes, at slumber parties. I'm sure you know it. It goes something like:
Where will we be in ten years?
What will they say about us?
What will so-and-so be doing?
Anyway, in case you want to know (in advance) the answers to those types of questions, I know what people will say, at least in part, about you...

They will say something like: She lives, she shines… and she makes a really good friend, too. (The best!)

You mean SO much to so many different people...

especially to Me.

Each day, you make my day
a little bit brighter.
In every way,
you make my smile
a little bit wider.
You came my way,
and I'm glad you stayed...

...because in every way
you make my life
a little bit brighter,
and I hope I do
the same for you.

# A True Friend

A friend is someone you turn to when you have no place to go... but a true friend is someone you stop and talk to when you have a million places to be, and yet... and yet... you want to see how they are. A friend is someone who tells you it will be okay...a true friend is someone who stays with you or calls until it is. A friend is like a day of fine, fine weather...A true friend reminds you that some days... the sky can be blue (even if it isn't right then).

A friend will meet you at the finish line... A true friend lights the way.

# A Friendship Flower:

Life is so uncertain —
so many people come and
go, like rain. But no
matter where I have stood
or what roads
I've been down,
you have been there for
me — at every turn,
along the way...

...and I guess
that some things
change and other
things don't and there are
some special
types of friendships
that grow and yet
stay the same.
And I'm just really glad
we've got that
special sort of
friendship...
that is there for you;
there for you always.

I forget a lot
of things...

My wallet, for instance...
or where I last put
my good set of keys. 

I forget addresses
and phone numbers, and
sometimes I even forget
the date.

I forget a lot
of things, and I
will forget a lot more
before this life is through.

But one thing I know
for sure, my friend...

...I will never forget you.

May your dreams
soar like kites...

May your hopes
fly high.

May you smile often
and love like there
is no tomorrow.

May all your tomorrows
be magic.

Through the years, the tears, the smiles, the miles...

...and all the things that happened while we were out there chasing our dreams...

In the end,
friends are what
matter most.

# Thanks for Being My Friend

Thanks for listening until the end.
For giving advice, and lending a hand.
For sticking around, and trying to understand.
For laughing with me.
And for sharing your life...

Thanks for being my friend.

Take this little book
and put it someplace
special so that every
time you look at it
you will remember just
how special you are...

and just how much
your friendship means
to me.